i explore

W9-APJ-390

POLAR ANIMALS

make
believe
ideas

WHAT'S INSIDE?

Discover more about amazing polar animals!

Polar life

Musk oxen

Arctic terns

Polar bears

Penguins

Weddell seals

Reindeer

Narwhals

Climate change

POLAR LIFE

Our planet has two polar regions – the Arctic and the Antarctic. They are the coldest places in the world.

Antarctic desert

i discover

The icy continent of Antarctica is a desert. It is much drier than even the Sahara Desert! Few animals live on the land, but many are able to survive in the freezing ocean.

Arctic

Arctic hare

North Pole

→ i learn ✕

The frozen land around
the Arctic Ocean is
called tundra. During
the harsh winters, only
certain animals and
plants can survive,
such as the Arctic hare,
but in summer, the
tundra supports a
wide variety of life.

Southern Ocean

Antarctica

Antarctic

Cloudberry plant in Arctic tundra

During summer at the poles, the sun stays low in the sky at night and does not set.

In winter, the sea around Antarctica freezes. This area of land and ice is so big that you could fit the United States inside it three times!

Polar summer

✔ Lives in the Arctic

POLAR BEARS

Class: Mammal

Polar bears are the largest meat-eating animals on land! With an amazing sense of smell and claws as sharp as a tiger's, they are awesome predators.

nose

Polar bear following a scent

⊗

🏠 | i fact 🔍

ⓘ Polar bears can smell a seal at its breathing hole from nearly 1 mile (1.6 km) away.

10

Under a polar bear's thick, snowy white fur, its skin is black! This black skin takes in extra heat from the Sun and helps it to keep warm in the freezing Arctic.

Polar bear swimming

thick fur

i discover

A polar bear can swim over 60 miles (100 km) without resting! Its front legs pull it forward and it uses its back legs to steer. It can also travel just by floating on the ice!

Polar bear floating on ice

back leg

front leg

PENGUINS

Class: Birds

Penguins are flightless
birds that live south
of the Equator.
Using their wings as
flippers, they are fast,
effective swimmers.

thick layers of feathers

→ i learn ✕

In winter, a female emperor
penguin lays her egg, then
goes to feed at sea for up to
two months. The male stays
behind with other males in
a group called a colony. He
balances the egg on his feet
and covers it with his warm,
feathery skin. This keeps the
egg warm until it hatches.

penguin chick

feet

Penguin swimming

i discover

Although they don't look it, penguins are camouflaged! When a penguin swims, its black back helps it blend in with the sea when seen from above, while its white belly helps it blend into the sky when seen from below.

wing

Galapagos penguin

i fact

Not all penguins live in the cold Antarctic. Galapagos penguins live near the Equator!

i explore MORE

King penguin
partners use their
own special calls
to find each other
in a colony.

i explore

✔ Lives in the Arctic

MUSK OXEN

skull bone

Class: Mammals

Musk oxen have existed for many thousands of years. They get their name from the musky scent males produce while searching for a female.

i discover

Musk oxen live and travel in a herd. If the herd is threatened by predators like wolves, it forms a tight pack to protect the young. Individuals may even charge down any would-be attackers.

horn

Musk oxen herd in a pack

ℹ️ Male musk oxen butt their heads together in fierce battles for territory and females. A layer of horn and skull bone 4 in (10 cm) thick protects the brain during these fights.

thick coat

➡️ **i learn** ❌

A musk ox is protected from the cold by two layers of thick hair. In summer, it sheds the thick underlayer to keep cool.

Musk ox with winter coat

WEDDELL SEALS

Class: Mammals

Weddell seals can cope with temperatures below -94°F (-70°C). They stay close to holes in the ice so they can shelter from winter storms and feed in the water.

whiskers

🏠 | **i fact** | 🔍

ⓘ A Weddell seal's whiskers are so sensitive that they can detect ripples from fish swimming past.

Killer whale hunting Weddell seal

i discover

Killer whales hunt Weddell seals. By staying on the ice joined to Antarctica's shore, the seals can avoid attack, but on drifting ice at sea they are vulnerable.

mouth

A Weddell seal's sharp, ice-grinding teeth

i learn

To make and maintain a breathing hole, a Weddell seal scrapes away the ice with its teeth. After years of scraping, a seal's teeth become so worn down that it cannot eat and eventually dies.

REINDEER

Class: Mammal

Reindeer, or caribou, have thick, warm coats and can travel huge distances across the Arctic tundra each year.

antler

nose

Reindeer

⌂ | i fact | 🔍

i Reindeer are the only species of deer where both males and females grow antlers.

A reindeer herd gives birth to most of its calves in a week. A day-old calf can run faster than a man but can still be killed by eagles, wolves, or bears.

Reindeer and calf

warm coat

➡ i learn ✕

A reindeer's large, hard hooves help to support its weight on the winter snow and make it easier to dig down to the ground for food. In summer, its feet soften so it can travel across marshland without sinking.

large hoof

21

During a year, a herd of reindeer can travel over 3,106 miles (5,000 km) to find food!

Herd of reindeer

✔ Lives in the Arctic
✔ Lives in the Antarctic

ARCTIC TERNS

Class: Birds

Over its lifetime, an Arctic tern can travel nearly a million miles as it flies from the Arctic to the Antarctic and back again.

Parent feeding chick

i discover

The Arctic tern nests and rears its chicks farther north than any other bird. By doing this it has 24 hours of sunlight in which to feed its young.

The Arctic tern has very long, pointed wings that are perfect for gliding and soaring over long distances. A long, forked tail helps the bird to turn quickly in the air.

○○●○○

long wing

tail

ⓘ Arctic terns never see winter because they travel from one end of the world to the other each year!

A tern hunts by hovering in the air while watching for fish in the sea below. To do this, it beats its wings quickly while keeping its head still.

Terns hunting ✕

»

NARWHALS

Class: Mammals

Narwhals are known as the unicorns of the sea because of the huge spiral tusk that males grow.

«   »

Narwhals swimming in ice passageways

⊗

i discover

Narwhals must surface to breathe every 30 minutes. They travel along long gaps in the ice while searching for food so they can reach the surface more easily.

i fact

Narwhals produce sounds that bounce off objects and echo back, telling them what is around them. This is called echolocation.

A male narwhal's tusk is actually an overgrown canine tooth! It can grow to 9 ft (2.7 m) long. Narwhals are often seen rubbing tusks, an activity called tusking.

tusk

CLIMATE CHANGE

Climate describes the general weather conditions of an area over many years. Recently, scientists have noticed that Earth's climates are changing.

»

🏠 | i facts | 🔍

Polar bears traveling

ⓘ Around 75% of the fresh water on Earth is currently in the Antarctic ice sheet.

● Climate change happens for many reasons, but we think that the fuels we use are part of the problem.

If climate change continues, the Earth will become warmer and its weather more extreme, with more flooding and droughts. It could also reduce the amount of ice in the polar regions.

○○●○○

Melting Antarctic ice

i discover

In the last 30 years, the size of the ice covering the Arctic has decreased dramatically, preventing animals from traveling across it to breed or find food. If this continues, animals such as polar bears could die out.

i explore FACTS

(i) Polar bears and penguins never meet in the wild, because polar bears live in the Arctic and penguins live south of the Equator.

True seals are different from fur seals and sea lions because they have no external ears and cannot hold themselves up on their front flippers.

Inuits call the musk ox "oomingmak," which means "bearded one."

The South Pole is on land, but the North Pole is on floating ice.

Emperor penguins huddle together in winter to keep warm. They constantly shuffle so the penguins on the cold edges of the colony get a turn in the middle.

Over 40 million years, the fish living in the Southern Ocean have adapted to the freezing water by developing a special antifreeze in their blood.